THE CHARM
NORTH CORNV

POLZEATH
AND SURROUNDING DISTRICTS

As Seen Through The Eyes Of Frank Maycock
Polzeath Photographer and Publisher

by

Alan Drew

Triskele Publications
1993

First published in 1993 by Triskele Publications
c/o 1 Cross Lane Gardens, Ticehurst, East Sussex TN5 7HY.

Copyright: Triskele Publications 1993

All rights reserved

ISBN 0 9520627 0 4

Printed by Lambda Business Services, East Grinstead, West Sussex.

FOR EACH BOOK SOLD

THE ROYAL MARSDEN CANCER FUND
203 FULHAM ROAD, LONDON SW3
(REGISTERED CHARITY NO. 274034)

WILL RECEIVE A £1.00 DONATION

CONTENTS

	Page
Introduction	7
Acknowledgements	8
Boscastle	9 – 10
Delabole	11
Bossiney	12
Tintagel	13 – 15
Trebarwith	16
Port Gaverne	17 – 18
Port Isaac	19 – 21
Port Quin	22 – 23
St. Endellion	24
Lundy Bay	25
Pentire & The Rumps	26 – 27
Polzeath	28 – 52
Greenaway Beach	53
Daymer Bay	54 – 55

CONTENTS
(continued)

	Page
St. Enodoc	56 – 57
Trebetherick	58
Rock	59 – 61
Tredrizzick	62
St. Minver	63
Chapel Amble	64
Wadebridge	65 – 66
Little Petherick	67
Padstow	68 – 72
Trevone	73 – 74
Trevose	75
Porthcothan	76
Harlyn Bay	77
Mother Ivey's Bay	78
'The Long Day Closes'	79
Bibliography	80

INTRODUCTION

Five years have elapsed since the idea for this book was first conceived when, whilst collecting postcards of the area in which I live, I found that cards of other counties were also available. In discovering cards of Cornwall, a childhood memory was re-kindled when I found identical examples of cards that I sent to family and friends some 25–30 years earlier. Not only that, but older cards from the same series could also be purchased and I discovered that the publisher of these cards, one Frank Maycock, had created a pictorial history of North Cornwall between 1915 and 1945 with over 850 different cards. Because I had spent so many of my school holidays in Polzeath, I felt the need to share my memories and affection of the area with those who also had a similar interest — hence this book.

Frank Maycock, it is believed, was born in 1885 and lived in Hall Green, Birmingham for the early part of his life. In 1918 he and his wife came to Polzeath where they rented property on Pentire. In 1921, they moved to more spacious rented accommodation, at West Ray in Trewint Valley, partly for the benefit of their two children, Rupert and Eva. Just one year later he established a shop called The Little Art and Bookshop in premises on the beach.

As the business developed, so they were able to afford to move to a new house which he had specially built for his family in 1935 — Avalon, on Tristram. While they were there they sold the Little Art Shop and later, in 1946, the house for £1,500.00, moving to Tewkesbury, Gloucestershire, for a couple of years. They returned to Polzeath to live at Morwenna, in Shilla Valley before leaving the district completely in 1949 to settle at Langport, Somerset.

I hope that much enjoyment is had in comparing some of the scenes of 70 years ago with those of today, and that people realise just how important these cards are for illustrating many scenes that can never again be re-created.

Alan Drew
Ticehurst
East Sussex

ACKNOWLEDGEMENTS

The author wishes to thank the many kind people who have offered guidance and assisted him with research and various pieces of information and memories from the past. In particular:

Mrs. M. Philp of Tristram, Polzeath

Mr. R. Hocking of Highcliffe, Polzeath

Mrs. E. Male of Trebetherick

Mr. R. Hoskins of Wadebridge

Mr. J. Burwood of Wadebridge

Mr. T. Sign of Orpington, Kent

and, last but not least,

My Wife and Family
who have supported me so well during
the past 18 months in such difficult circumstances,
also
a special note of thanks to the staff at
The Royal Marsden Hospital, Sutton, Surrey.

BOSCASTLE FROM NEW ROAD (1923)

At first glance, one might say that little about this view has changed today from 70 years ago but looking at the properties behind the bridge to the right of the road, the premises beyond what is now the Riverside Hotel have been demolished and the entire area re-developed over the years to include new shops and flats with a large car-park. The 'New Road' was constructed in about 1920.

472 Boscastle Harbour

BOSCASTLE HARBOUR (1928)

It is quite difficult to imagine how large vessels managed to navigate their way into Boscastle Harbour with its twisting, turning channel but, with the assistance of horses and ropes from the adjacent paths, they reached their mooring place. Until the railway station at Camelford opened in 1893, most of the supplies for the village arrived by ship. The inner jetty was built in the late 1500's, funded by a local merchant. The outer jetty, rebuilt in 1962 after being destroyed by a mine, dates back to the early 19th century.

Prince of Wales at Delabole Slate Quarries. June 1927.

PRINCE OF WALES AT DELABOLE SLATE QUARRIES
(10th June 1927)

On the final day of his tour of the West Country in 1927, the Prince firstly visited the Delabole Slate Quarries and then Camelford, to inaugurate the new North Cornwall Water Supply works at Lower Moor. On arrival at the Quarry he was introduced to eight veterans of the pit whose combined ages totalled over 600 years and whose service there totalled 400 years. Prior to descending into the pit, the Prince observed seven charges being let-off at the east face of the pit, releasing tons of slate as a result. Interestingly, the pit employed some 450–500 men at this time.

370 Bossiney Garage and Tea Rooms

BOSSINEY GARAGE AND TEA ROOMS (1925)
Motorists tend to overlook Bossiney when travelling between Tintagel and Boscastle as there is very little to be seen here. Since this picture was taken, the properties have been altered considerably. The premises serving as a Garage and Tea Rooms have closed down and are now the Village Stores. Beyond here is one of the village's oldest properties, Bossiney Farm, which was built in 1571.

TREVENA VILLAGE, TINTAGEL (1922)

Although known as Tintagel nowadays, the village was known as Trevena, within the parish of Tintagel. Other villages in this parish included Treknow, Trebarwith and Bossiney. The Wharncliffe Arms Hotel, as it is now called, is named after a former local politician and landowner, whilst Trevena House, to the right of the hotel, now serves as 'King Arthur's Great Halls'. The shop further down on the right used to trade under the name of 'The Central Supply Stores' and was later extended, resulting in alterations to the house fronted by a glazed porch.

OLD POST OFFICE, TINTAGEL (1921)
Prior to becoming known as the Post Office, all letters etc. were delivered by messenger from Camelford. It was not until 1844 that the Post Office rented a room in the property for collection and distribution of mail within the area. This arrangement lasted until 1892. In 1895, the property was auctioned and subsequently bought by a group of artists who were unable to meet the high cost of renovation and in 1900, it was passed on to The National Trust who have maintained it ever since.

BEACH AND CASTLE RUINS, TINTAGEL (1922)
The Castle was built about 1145 by Reginald, Earl of Cornwall, and illegitimate son of Henry I. For 300 years the site was repaired and extended but eventually became derelict after the gap between the island and the mainland widened so much that it became impossible to cross. Another 400 years were to elapse before a new path was laid to the island and some repairs made to the Castle. As for King Arthur, his connection with the castle is only legendary, given that he is more closely linked with the end of the 5th Century.

145. "WE'VE HAD OUR PHOTOGRAPH TAKEN AT TREBARWITH"

WE'VE HAD OUR PHOTOGRAPH TAKEN AT TREBARWITH (1921)

Slate quarrying began here in 1490 and continued until the early part of this century. The usual method for obtaining the slate was to blast the rock whilst the tide was in, and collect it when the tide had receded. These donkeys on the beach were not here to give rides to children as one might expect but were regularly employed to carry sand for agricultural use on the local farms. Because of the rocky approach to the beach, carts could not be used here unlike other bays around North Cornwall. At Polzeath, a donkey and cart employed for the same purpose used to earn 1/6d (7.5p) per load and take up to six loads per day.

117. PORT GAVERNE, NORTH CORNWALL

PORT GAVERNE, NORTH CORNWALL (1921)

Although Fishing and Boat-Building were the main trades of the village, the busiest times were during the 19th Century when Delabole Slate was exported from here. The Port Gaverne Hotel, formerly the village inn, dates back to the 15th Century and was very popular with the crews of the incoming vessels.

729 The Haven, Port Gaverne.

THE HAVEN, PORT GAVERNE (1936)
The main building in this picture, the Headlands Hotel, is fronted by a narrow lane that was once known as the Great Slate Road. It was laid in 1807 by the Delabole Slate Company to permit easier access to the Port, but because of the steep descent, the drivers of the carts would deliberately steer into the wall in order to slow the vehicles down. A track opposite the Hotel led to the former quay-side, the remains of which can be seen in this picture, behind the two boats.

QUAINT PORT ISAAC (1925)

Dolphin Street, the subject of this picture, gets its name from the old Dolphin Inn, now called Dolphin Cottage. It can be reached from Fore Street by way of Temple Bar and 'Squeeze-ee-Belly Alley', so-called because of the narrow way, just 18" wide, that passes alongside Temple Cottage. Note the children in this photograph, one of whom (on the right) is bare-footed.

164 Port Isaac Harbour and Village

PORT ISAAC HARBOUR AND VILLAGE (1922)
Pilchard fishing was the main industry of the village until the beginning of the Second World War. Many went for export after being stored and salted in the old fish cellars. After the war, Herring became the main catch but nowadays Mackerel and Shellfish are most abundant. Severe flooding in the lower part of the town was a frequent occurrence prior to the construction of the two breakwaters in the mid-1920's

A TIGHT FIT WITH THE LIFEBOAT AT PORT ISAAC (1925)

When Port Isaac received its first lifeboat in 1869, it was housed in the building that is now known as the Post Office. These premises were used until 1927 when a more suitable place was built opposite the slipway on The Platt although that was closed six years later. Very occasionally, when tides were difficult at Port Isaac, the lifeboat was hauled to Port Quin by oxen or horses to be launched there. At the bottom of Fore Street, the buildings on the inside corner still show signs of rope friction from hauling the vessel up and down the steep hill.

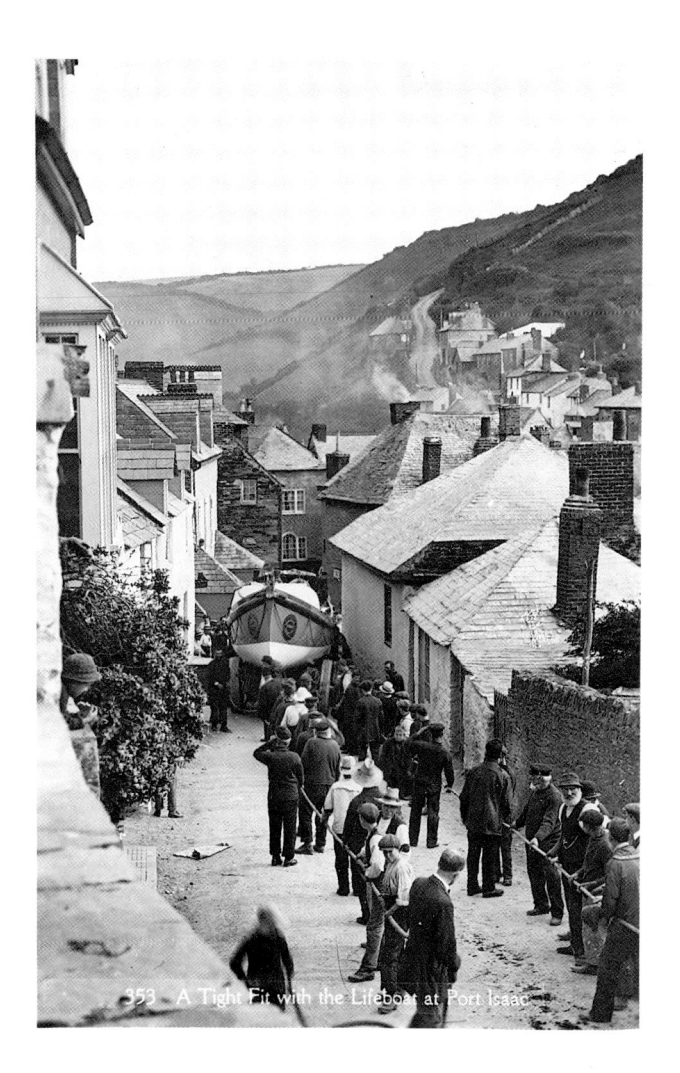

748 Port Quin Village.

PORT QUIN VILLAGE (1937)
Legend has it that in 1697, the entire Port Quin fishing fleet was destroyed in a storm and all of the fishermen drowned. The remaining inhabitants, most of them women, moved to Port Isaac or beyond for security and for employment. By 1850, the population of the village was larger than had ever been recorded previously but the fish stocks dwindled and the village became derelict once more until The National Trust took over some of the properties and restored them for use as holiday cottages.

PORT QUIN, HAVEN (1930)

Port Quin's most recent claim to fame is when it was used as a filming location by the BBC for their 1970's series called Poldark. Behind the slipway, in the centre of the picture, can be seen the old Fish Cellars and on the right are Quin Farm Cottage and Trevose House. Out of picture and high above the harbour on the south cliff-top is the battlemented folly of Doyden Castle that was built in the eighteenth century and financed, apparently, on the proceeds of gambling.

ST. ENDELLION CHURCH (1927)

The Church and Parish are named after St. Endelienta, the twenty-first daughter of the Welsh King Brechanus, and sister of St. Mabyn, St. Menefreda, St. Nectan, St. Tudy and others. Built in 1260 it was, like most Cornish Churches, enlarged in the fifteenth century and now consists of nave, chancel and two aisles with their chapels. The tower was added later, reputedly built by Bristol merchants to serve as a landmark, and at 480′ above sea-level it can be seen from many miles around.

327 Lundy Beach at Low Tide, near Polzeath

LUNDY BEACH AT LOW TIDE (1924)
One of the lesser used beaches on this part of the Cornish Coast, Lundy Bay is only accessible at low-tide but is well worth a visit and taking a picnic to, if the weather forecast for the day is favourable! Around the corner of the first headland visible in this picture is Port Quin. From the Coastal Footpath that runs behind Lundy Bay can be seen a natural arch in the cliffs which, at high tide, can provide quite spectacular wave effects.

562 Rumps Point, Pentire

RUMPS POINT, PENTIRE (1929)
Cliffe Castle, on the east side of The Rumps, dates back to the Iron Age. Previous excavations here have revealed foundations of several huts together with the remains of animal bones and pottery. Despite these findings, it is thought unlikely that there was ever any permanent occupation of this site. A local theory suggests that it was connected in some way with King Arthur's battles.

A QUIET RESTING PLACE ON PENTIRE CLIFFS (1929)

The views around Pentire and The Rumps can be magnificent at any time of the year though Spring and early Summer give visitors that little bit more in terms of colour from the abundance of wild plants that abound here. Also noticeable is the variety of bird-life and, on occasions, the presence of some seals on the rocks below. At one time, parts of Pentire were mined by a company called The Pentire Glaze and Pentire United Silver-Lead Mines. Little evidence remains of these workings today.

549. A Quiet Resting Place on Pentire Cliff

POLZEATH BAY (1920)

Taken in about 1920, this picture clearly shows how unspoilt Polzeath was 70 years ago. The postman on his cart would have come from Wadebridge to deliver the mail. The large building in the centre of the picture had been built 2 years earlier and served as garaging and workshops, owned by Mr. Couch who lived in the cottage to the extreme right. Up the hill on the corner towards Highcliffe can be seen the old Methodist Chapel, built in 1911 and below that on the opposite side of the road is the old Post Office which also served as the village stores. The small shed-like building in the foreground was a tea-room, also run by the Couch family.

A SUMMER'S MORNING (1926)
Several years after the previous picture was taken, the new Post Office Stores has been built although not yet opened for business. To the extreme right, the end cottage has been rebuilt and converted to serve as a new shop for the Couch family. The Charabanc would have come from Wadebridge en-route to Polzeath and Rock as part of the regular, twice-daily, bus service for the area.

466 Beach Approach, Polzeath

BEACH APPROACH (1928)
In 1927 the Post Office Stores, owned by F. Male, opened for business and was selling 'BP' Petrol in direct competition with Couch's (Shell) Garage opposite. Looking towards the far side of the bay, the house on the left of the Village Street (Skippers Cottage) has been modernised and had a taller first-floor storey added to it. Signs of development on Highcliffe (Gullsway) are also evident at the top left of the picture.

POLZEATH LODGE HOTEL (1939)
When originally built in about 1900, the property was nothing like as large as it appears in this picture. Three or four additional extensions were erected in the first 30 years after its construction. Nowadays the property is known as the Pinewood Flats, having been converted in the late 1950's. The vegetable gardens also belonged to the Hotel though these have long since disappeared with the arrival of the Caravan Park and the Coronation Gardens.

105 POLZEATH POST OFFICE

POLZEATH POST OFFICE (1921)
Prior to 1913, this property was known locally as the old Account Office after its connection with the local Lead & Silver mines at Pentire, the last of which ceased to work in the 1860's. Until 1927 it served as the Post Office Stores when the business transferred to the larger premises seen in the previous pictures. More recently, the upper part of the property has been converted for residential use whilst the lower floor is named The Galleon Cafe.

16. Chapel Corner, Polzeath

CHAPEL CORNER (1920)

Known now as Smugglers Cottage, the building on the right of the picture has survived for over 250 years. In 1983 part of the internal structure of the building was altered and in the Living Room was found an original Cornish Cloam Oven that had been bricked-in during a previous re-decorating project. The photographer would have been standing on the steps of the old Post Office to take this picture.

17 The Village Street, Polzeath

THE VILLAGE STREET (1920)
When this picture was taken, there were very few motor cars around to create traffic problems. The quaintness of this picture is over-shadowed by the newer buildings of New Polzeath, where some new bungalows were just beginning to spread eastwards beyond Atlantic Terrace.

641 The Village Street, Polzeath.

THE VILLAGE STREET (1933)
Even today, the road at this point can present problems to some drivers of larger vehicles, despite the widening scheme of 60 years ago! Major alterations to some of the cottages are apparent when comparing this picture with the previous one. Also, development on the New Polzeath side continues, where more houses and bungalows have been built.

120 THE FOOTBRIDGE, POLZEATH BEACH

THE FOOTBRIDGE, POLZEATH BEACH (1921)
Although perfectly safe to cross when the tide was out, the footbridge would occasionally get washed away in the high, winter tides. Behind the bridge, to the right, can be seen the 'Road' crossing where drivers had to steer their way through the stream. This sometimes led to them becoming stuck in the sand, allowing the younger inhabitants of the village to earn a little pocket-money by assisting the hapless drivers!

835. The New Road, Polzeath.

THE NEW ROAD (1939)
The Village Street was widened in 1932 which involved the demolition of the original Methodist Chapel. The new Chapel, built just 50 yards away, opened on the 15th April 1933. Services in the interim period were held in the Tea Rooms above F. Male's Village Stores. The Road Bridge was constructed in 1934. All of the houses in the Village Street, with the exception of Smugglers Cottage, have either been modernised or extended. Car-parking on the beach cost just 6d (2.5p)!

803 A Summers Day at Polzeath.

A SUMMERS DAY AT POLZEATH (1938)
The new block of shops in the centre of this picture were built in 1935, replacing the wooden hut that served as the Couch's Tea Rooms. To the left of the picture are the lock-up garages also belonging to Couch's though these were converted to holiday chalets in the early 1950's. The small white building fronting the beach is The Little Art Shop. Points worth noting in this picture are the ice-cream van (centre-left of picture) and the cars on the beach, most of which are black though a few variations in colour can be seen.

POLZEATH BEACH (1939)
The premises belonging to F. Male is now selling Shell Petroleum (see earlier picture No.466) and the GPO has installed a Public Telephone box outside his shop. To the right of the picture is The Little Art Shop which was run by Frank Maycock, photographer and publisher of all the illustrations in this book. His premises were built in 1922 and demolished in 1966 to be replaced by the present buildings.

SHILLA MILL (1925)

Shilla Mill dates back to the early 1590's and was, until 1885, a prosperous grist (corn for grinding) mill. Subsequently, the building was converted into living accommodation with many of its beams being taken from the local wrecks. It is also believed that the property was a haven for smugglers and this is made even more likely by the presence of a cave-opening nearby. The donkey in the picture was owned by the then resident of the mill house, a Mr Chudleigh, and in winter months he would allow her inside the house to keep warm! The property has been considerably modernised since this picture was taken.

80 THE OLD RUSTIC BRIDGE BY THE MILL. SHILLA MILL, POLZEATH.

THE OLD RUSTIC BRIDGE BY THE MILL (1920)

Although the bridge still survives, the river is considerably narrower now. With the foliage that exists there today, it is almost impossible to see the mill house from the bridge. A large stone slab which spans the stream near the bridge bears evidence of great antiquity and was probably retrieved from the adjacent hillside. The area to the left of the picture, behind the trees, now forms the perimeter of the Valley Caravan Park.

178 Pentire Point from Trebetherick Hill.

PENTIRE POINT FROM TREBETHERICK HILL (1922)
The area around Pentire and The Rumps was taken over by the National Trust in the early 1930's. Without the Trust, how many holiday bungalows might have been built on the Headland by now? The entrance to the right of the picture would be to The Polzeath Lodge Hotel and the house lower down the hill is Ivy Cottage.

POLZEATH FROM TRENANT VALLEY (1924)

The house in the foreground was built in 1908 and named 'West Ray'. Not only was this house rented by Frank Maycock in later years, but he also used the name of the house for many of his postcards and called them the 'West Ray Series'. In this picture, a lack of buildings on Tristram and Highcliffe is clearly evident.

832 Reflections on Polzeath Beach.

REFLECTIONS ON POLZEATH BEACH (1939)
This late-1930's picture shows the development that has taken place in Trenant Valley during the 20 or so years since the previous picture was taken. To the left can be seen the original Beach Shop in the guise of a small shed-like structure. The building now on this site and occupied by Surfside Too was built in the late 1940's.

692 The Blow Hole, Polzeath.

THE BLOW HOLE, POLZEATH (1935)
Watching the Atlantic Rollers break across the rocks while the wind howls and sends a huge spray of salt water across the cliff-top is just one of nature's many simple attractions that can be found in and around the area of Polzeath.

337 Toilers of the Sea, Polzeath

TOILERS OF THE SEA (1924)
The text on the back of the postcard could have been written by any one of the children in this picture, or the countless thousands of others that have played in this pool by the Beach Steps over the years:

'Wonderful spot for a holiday. Bathing all day. Weather extremely hot. Going home on Saturday and back to school next week — worst luck.'

200. ATLANTIC TERRACE, POLZEATH.

ATLANTIC TERRACE (1922)

When the first bricks of Atlantic Terrace were laid in 1898, it is unlikely that much consideration was given by the developers regarding cliff erosion. Considerable reinforcements were laid at the foot of the cliffs here in the early 1980's, in an effort to stem the problem. The iron railings would probably have been removed in the early 1940's for the war effort. The Atlantic House Hotel, at the far end of the terrace, has occupied the same site for the past 90 years.

GREYSTONES PRIVATE HOTEL (1929)
Built in the late 1920's, this property remained generally unaltered until quite recently when a new conservatory was added to the side of the property. It is now called, perhaps more appropriately, the Pentire Rocks Hotel.

NEW POLZEATH (1926)
This part of New Polzeath, close to the National Trust area of Pentire, has not been able to develop so rapidly as that of Old Polzeath. In this picture, no buildings have been built on the grass square in the middle of the other houses and the area remains much the same today.

POLZEATH FROM MINIVER HILL (1928)
This late 1920's photo is intended for comparison with the following photograph to illustrate how progress changed the face of Polzeath and, in particular, on Highcliffe and Tristram Field.

724 Polzeath, General View.

POLZEATH — GENERAL VIEW (1936)
Considerable alterations and additions are evident when comparing this picture with the previous one. The road down to the bay has been widened causing the Methodist Chapel to be re-sited. The Polzeath Lodge Hotel (now Pinewood Flats) has had an extension added to it and the Polzeath Hotel, further up the hill, has been built. The new block of shops can also be seen to the left of the picture. Development on Tristram Field and Highcliffe has begun to gather pace, though post-war development was more rapid and, as we can see today, the entire area is awash with houses and bungalows.

51

342 The New Tennis Courts, Polzeath

THE NEW TENNIS COURTS (1925)
A lovely picture from the early 1920's before the area became engulfed with houses and bungalows. Built for the Atlantic House Hotel in 1922, the courts were used for recreation until 1938 when the area was given over to car-parking — probably a more profitable source of income.

876 Wrecked "Media" on Greenaway Rocks.

WRECKED 'MEDIA' ON GREENAWAY ROCKS (1939)

Built at Middlesborough in 1915 as a mine-laying vessel, HMS Media had served its duty and was being towed to South Wales for scrapping when, on the 28th January 1939, it broke loose from its towing line whilst passing Trevose Head during a severe hurricane. Four crew were on board at the time, one of whom got swept overboard whilst the remaining three were saved by the Trebetherick coastguard team using the breeches-buoy. Very little remains of the wreck now.

797 Daymer from Bray Hill.

DAYMER FROM BRAY HILL (1938)
Like Polzeath, development around Daymer Bay began in the early 1920's although many of the properties that exist today were built after the Second World War. Daymer House and Daymer Bay House can be seen in the foreground. The bay itself, popular for its sheltered position, actually conceals a submarine forest that was first discovered about 200 years ago when a displacement of sand revealed the roots and trunks of trees such as oak, yew, and some soft-wooded trees.

11 Daymer Bay and St. Enodoc Church

DAYMER BAY AND ST. ENODOC CHURCH (1920)

Although the Golf Course had been established for some 30 years before this picture was taken, the marshes were left untouched from any re-development scheme. The church, which dates back to the Norman period when it was a chapel, received its tower and spire in the 13th Century, and the south aisle in the 15th Century. Later to be covered by the sand dunes when it suffered considerable damage, it was not until 1863/4 that restoration was accomplished and the church has seen regular services since. More recently, it has been the burial place of the Poet Laureate, Sir John Betjeman.

211 LIFE SAVING ROCKET AT ST. ENODOC

LIFE-SAVING ROCKET AT ST. ENODOC (1922)
The local Coastguards from Trebetherick used to practice regularly with the Life Saving Apparatus, using part of the St. Enodoc Golf Links for this purpose. The rocket, to which a rope was attached, was capable of travelling hundreds of yards and would, under emergency conditions, be targeted to travel over and beyond the vessel in distress thereby ensuring that the rope was reachable. This equipment and method of transport was replaced in the mid-1930's.

PRINCE OF WALES PLAYING ON ST. ENODOC GOLF LINKS (1927)
The old wooden clubhouse was first constructed in 1890, rebuilt in 1907 and existed until 1937 when the new clubhouse opened, in time for the English Ladies Close Championship of that year. This picture depicts the Prince of Wales playing golf whilst on a visit to North Cornwall in June 1927 after travelling from Truro where he had officiated at the opening ceremonies of the annual County Agricultural Show. The Prince was the President of St. Enodoc Golf Club from 1928 until King George V died.

638 Daymer Lane, Trebetherick.

DAYMER LANE, TREBETHERICK (1933)
The building on the extreme left of the picture was home to the first Telephone Exchange in Trebetherick. The sloping-roof extension was the Post Office premises. Since 1960, a considerable number of alterations have taken place at this junction, including the widening of the Polzeath — Wadebridge road, the demolition of the garages to the left of the old Telephone Exchange and the widening of Daymer Lane outside the Post Office. Note, in the distance, the trail of steam from a train heading towards Padstow.

ROCK POST OFFICE AND HOTEL (1920)

Built in 1895, the Rock Hotel survived until 1978 when, together with the cottages behind the Post Office, it was demolished to make way for a new hotel called The Mariner's, which opened a year later. None of the buildings in this picture, even the stores to the left of the slipway, now exist. The old Custom House (in name only and formerly used for storing of coal and grain) at the end of the quay-side, was saved from demolition when, in 1976, it was renovated and subsequently used by the Rock Sailing Club.

260. Rock Beach from the Sandhills.

ROCK BEACH FROM THE SANDHILLS (1923)
Why call this area Rock when, apart from the more recent deposits of rock on the seashore, the entire beach area is predominantly sand? Well, originally it was called Black-Tor or Black-Rock after a nearby hill upon which a black head of Greenstone appears through the sand. The area in the foreground has since been severely landscaped to allow for the development of holiday homes, retail premises and a car-park.

SUNNY LANE, ROCK (1939)
Surprisingly, the cottages to the left of the road remain virtually unaltered since the day that this picture was taken although the trees to the front of them have been felled, the heavy wooden gates have disappeared and the road at this point has been slightly widened.

328 A Little Grey Home in the West, Tredrizzick Bridge

A LITTLE GREY HOME IN THE WEST, TREDRIZZICK BRIDGE (1924)
Although the mode of transport in this picture is an early example of a moped, quite a few cyclists must have rested on this wall before facing the short but steep climb up the hill to St. Minver. The house shown here, Hill Cottage, was totally rebuilt about 6 years ago but retains most of its original outline.

243 St. Minver Village.

ST. MINVER VILLAGE (1923)
The parish of St. Minver is widely spread and takes in such villages as Trevanger, Tredrizzick, Pitomy, Penmain and Stoptide. The village itself has no great claim to fame though the Church dates back to the Norman period. Its steeple, at 115' high, can be seen from miles around and was, until recently, charted as a day-mark for vessels at sea and could not be altered in any way without due permission from the Board of Trade.

841 Chapel Amble.

CHAPEL AMBLE (1939)
Time was when a barge could be taken (rowed) at high tide all the way to Amble from the River Camel by passing under Trewornan Bridge where the Wadebridge-Polzeath road crosses the creek. A land reclamation scheme in the late 1960's prevents such journeys from being made now.

15TH CENTURY BRIDGE, WADEBRIDGE (1928)

The original bridge was built in the reign of Edward IV, the cost for which was raised by a Mr Thomas Loveybond, the Vicar of Egloshayle. Completed in 1485, it was originally 17 arches wide, measured 320' in length and was just 9' wide. In 1852 the bridge was widened leaving 13 arches visible. The remaining four arches were built over, supporting the four shops on the south-east side of the bridge. Further widening took place in 1962/3, its character and appearance being preserved.

310 Wadebridge Town Hall

WADEBRIDGE TOWN HALL (1924)

The Town Hall was built in 1888, at a cost of £3,000. It was built from local stone, designed to contain up to 600 people in the Main Hall. Two items of some interest inside the building are a large stained-glass window that was presented by Viscount Clifden and also the Arms of the Molesworth family of nearby Pencarrow. The Co-operative stores next to the Town Hall are now occupied by the NSS newsagents whilst the cottages to the other side were demolished in the early 1930's.

612. A Cornish Village, Little Petherick.

A CORNISH VILLAGE, LITTLE PETHERICK (1933)

Still as quaint today as when this picture was taken in 1933, Little Petherick is situated 2 miles east of Padstow on the banks of a creek on the River Camel. At the river end of the creek stands the Old Iron Bridge that used to carry the railway line from Padstow to Wadebridge but more recently has been converted to a footpath and cycle-way. Below the bridge can be seen the remains of one of Cornwall's 20 or so Tide Mills. It was the construction of the railway in the 1890's that led to its destruction.

PADSTOW HARBOUR (1927)

In this picture, part of the quay-side has just been completed. On the hill can be seen the (now) Metropole Hotel, built in 1898 at a cost of £12,000 and named the South Western Hotel — a connection to the recent construction of the railway which opened just a year later. Note the freight wagons on the quay-side, which were emptied of china clay for export to Ireland, whilst special fish wagons would be loaded constantly with Herrings and other fish for delivery to the Billingsgate Market in London. To the left of the picture, the ferry from Rock can be seen arriving.

154. PADSTOW FROM ABOVE STATION

PADSTOW FROM ABOVE STATION (1921)

The line from Wadebridge was opened in March 1899, the station being situated 260 miles from Waterloo Station, from where the famous Atlantic Coast Express commenced its journey to North Cornwall. Although holiday traffic on summer Saturdays was quite brisk, it was certainly not enough to 'balance the books' and after freight services ceased in 1965, the line closed completely in January 1967. The track-bed now survives as a footpath, aptly named 'The Camel Trail'.

207 Old Abbey House, Padstow

THE ABBEY HOUSE, PADSTOW (1922)

Also known locally as The Leper House, the property is believed to be the oldest in Padstow, apart from the Church, and dates back to Elizabethan times. From the cellar, a concealed tunnel is supposed to lead to the Squires House at Prideaux Place that was used by Charles II to escape from the Roundheads, by boat, to France. In 1938 the property was bought by a Mr & Mrs Simpson. He was from the family that owned the well-known shop 'Simpsons of the Strand' in London, though he died shortly after moving in. Many years later, Mrs Simpson became quite renowned herself for expressing her opinions in a very stern manner from the balcony of the house to the fascinated crowd below.

198. STEAM LIFEBOAT, "HELEN PEELE," in Padstow Harbour.

STEAM LIFEBOAT 'HELEN PEELE', IN PADSTOW HARBOUR (1922)
When not out on a mission, the Helen Peele lifeboat spent most of its time moored, always with steam-up, in Hawker's Cove. Introduced to Padstow in 1901, she invariably acted as a Tug to the sailing lifeboat 'Edmund Harvey' for getting the latter to sea in bad conditions. During her working life, she was involved with the rescue of 78 lives when assisting sister rescue ships and also saved another 10 lives on her own. She was withdrawn from service in 1929.

68 COASTGUARD STATION, HAWKER'S COVE, NEAR PADSTOW   "WEST RAY SERIES"

COASTGUARD STATION, HAWKER'S COVE (1920)
When the cottages in Hawker's Cove were built, they were specifically for use by Coastguards (left terrace) and Pilotmen (right terrace). After falling into a state of disrepair, they were renovated and restored for use as Council houses and holiday cottages. The Coastguard Station can be seen in the centre of the picture.

509 The Cot and Rose Cottage, Trevone

THE COT AND ROSE COTTAGE, TREVONE (1928)
On the left of this picture is The Cot Tearooms which, prior to opening in the early 1920's, was the Wesleyan Mission Chapel. In one local travel guide, the tearooms were described as 'the place where a rest and a daintily-served tea may be assured'. Rose Cottage was, for a short time, used as a Guest House, though both properties are now individual domestic residences.

622 Trevone Beach and Bungalows.

TREVONE BEACH AND BUNGALOWS (1933)
Like Polzeath, development in Trevone began in the 1920's. Its close proximity to Padstow, together with its own natural charm made it a pleasing resort for holidaymakers. Popular spots here include the Marble Cliffs, Tregudda Gorge and the sandy bay of Porthmissen.

TREVOSE LIGHTHOUSE & FOGHORN (1932)

After several previous proposals for its construction in 1809, 1813 and 1832 had been declined, the lighthouse was finally built in 1847. The tower is 87′ high and the light has an intensity of 770,000 candela with a range of 25 miles. The trumpet-like fog-horn measured 36′ in length and was built as an experiment in 1913, surviving until its removal in 1964.

589 Trevose Lighthouse and Foghorn

91 PORTHCOTHAN BEACH, NEAR PADSTOW   West Ray Series

PORTHCOTHAN BEACH, NEAR PADSTOW (1920)
As with all of the other coastal villages in the North Cornwall area (except Port Quin), Porthcothan has not escaped from random housing developments. The house in the centre of the picture is known as Beach Cottage and is shown prior to an additional cottage being built to the right of it, in the early 1930's. The main road now occupies the position where the horse is grazing.

225. HARLYN BAY.

HARLYN BAY (1923)

Harlyn Bay Prehistoric Cemetery was founded by a local property developer, Mr Reddie Mallett, in August 1900, whilst excavating foundations for a new house. After the discovery, he published a book and various postcards of the cemetery and surrounding area. The contents were initially housed in a small building nearby and later transferred to the Royal Institution of Cornwall Museum in Truro. On occasions, the Padstow lifeboat was launched from here after being hauled from Hawkers Cove by a team of horses.

585 Mother Ivey's Bay, looking South

MOTHER IVEY'S BAY, LOOKING SOUTH (1932)
This area was originally known as Polventon, but a local Trevone farm owner, widowed, by the name of Mother Ivey, insisted that she had sole rights to all wreckage in the bay which nobody disputed. Since 1967, the Padstow lifeboat has been stationed here.

31 "The Long Day Closes"—Evening at Polzeath

'THE LONG DAY CLOSES' (1920)
Another day over and, for some, a matter of packing all of their belongings back into their cases going home tomorrow. For others, it will be their first day which, with luck, will bring another gloriously sun-baked and cloudless sky.

Polzeath and the surrounding district may not be the picturesque and peaceful place that existed 60–70 years ago, but there is still plenty of charm around it that many people may be able to share for decades to come, as long as the local planners place beauty and nature before bricks and mortar.

BIBLIOGRAPHY

HISTORY OF TINTAGEL, William Taylor, 1927.
THE STORY OF PORT ISAAC, PORT QUIN & PORT GAVERNE, Monica Winstanley, 1973.
PADSTOW AND DISTRICT, Donald R. Rawe, 1984.
A SHORT GUIDE TO PORT ISAAC, Robin Penna, 1991.
PADSTOW AND DISTRICT GUIDE, 1959.
THE CHARM OF NORTH CORNWALL, F.A. Maycock, 1922.
TINTAGEL CASTLE OFFICIAL GUIDE, 1935.